Taking Mesopotamia

Jenny Lewis trained as a painter at the
Ealing School of Art before reading
Oxford. She is a poet, playwright
had plays and poetry cycles perform
including her verse drama, *After Gilgamesh* (for Pegasus
Oxford, published by Mulfran Press, 2011). She teaches poetry
at Oxford University.

Also by Jenny Lewis from Carcanet/Oxford*Poets*

Fathom

Jenny Lewis *Jenny Lewis* 4/08/2014

Taking Mesopotamia

To Elaine & Timmy
with love from

Jenny xx

Oxford*Poets*

CARCANET

First published in Great Britain in 2014 by
Carcanet Press Limited
Alliance House
Cross Street
Manchester M2 7AQ

www.carcanet.co.uk

A CIP catalogue record for this book is available from the British Library

ISBN 978 1 90618 811 5

The publisher acknowledges financial assistance from Arts Council England

Typeset by XL Publishing Services, Exmouth
Printed and bound in England by SRP Ltd, Exeter

For Gillian, Tom and Ed, with love

Contents

Arabic translations

Second Lieutenant T.C. Lewis

Preface

I

This book started with research into my father's part in the Mesopotamian campaign of World War I as a Second Lieutenant in the 4th Battalion, the South Wales Borderers (SWB), now the Royal Regiment of Wales. He was born in Blaenclydach and qualified as an analytical chemist aged 16, having served a year's apprenticeship with the Trehafod Colliery Laboratory. After his SWB commission (recommended by the Military Education Committee of the University College of South Wales) he was sent with his regiment to Mesopotamia (Iraq) in May 1916. While there he took over sixty photographs with a Box Brownie camera, some of which are published for the first time in this book. He was wounded at Kut-al-Amara on 11 January 1917 in bright moonlight, while on a covering party, and was invalided to Deolali, India. He remained in India for eighteen months, part of the time recuperating in the palace of the Maharajah of Jaipur. He later trained as a doctor (the first person in his family to go to university). Much later in his life he met my mother and they had two children, my sister Gillian and myself. He died of a coronary thrombosis when I was a few months old and I have been searching for him ever since.

The parallels I have been able to draw with recent wars in Iraq through monitoring news coverage and interviewing British, American and Iraqi soldiers, poets and commentators have provided me with valuable insights. Throughout the process I have been mindful of the fact that, in another era, the young men killed and wounded could have included my own two sons, Tom and Edward. I have tried to give the diary poems a loose narrative structure not always consonant with actual dates and times, although most of the content is based on fact.

II

The Anglo-Persian Oil Company was set up in 1909 after oil

fields had been discovered in Iraq, then known as Mesopotamia, meaning the land 'between two rivers' – the Tigris and Euphrates. Two years later, Winston Churchill, then First Sea Lord, bought a controlling stake in the company for Britain for £2.2 million.

The day after war was declared in 1914 a force of British and Indian troops landed in Southern Iraq to protect the pipeline that ran from Shushtar (Iran) to the refinery at Abadan on the Shatt-al-Arab river. The Indian Expeditionary Force D was the largest Indian Army force to serve abroad in World War I.

So began one of the most ill-fated, under-funded campaigns in British military history, and another chapter in the story of the great civilisations of the Ancient Near East, which were the first to divide the hour into 60 minutes and the circle into 360 degrees, the first to develop agriculture and the first to develop writing (originally pictograms, then cuneiform).

As well as the glorious achievements of the early Meso-potamians, their history, like ours, is chequered with hubris and empire-building – both of which themes can be found in the Sumerian *Epic of Gilgamesh*, dating from 2700 BC. This poem, first discovered by Victorian archaeologists on clay tablets in excavated libraries at historic sites such as Ur, Babylon and Nineveh, is the oldest piece of written literature in the world and fragments of it are still being brought to light.

Acknowledgements

Firstly, many thanks to Keiren Phelan and Arts Council South East for the generous grant which enabled this work. A Hawthornden Fellowship in June 2012 gave me time for final editing. The Imperial War Museum, the National Archives and the South Wales Borderers Museum have all greatly assisted my research, as has Nadia Atia's insightful manuscript *War in the Cradle of Civilisation*; also illuminating have been C.T. Atkinson's *The History of the South Wales Borderers: The Great War, 1914–1918* (Ray Westlake Military Books, 1999); Ron Wilcox's *Battles on the Tigris* (Pen and Sword, 2006); and A.R. George's translation of *The Epic of Gilgamesh* (Allen Lane, the Penguin Press, 1999.)

Many thanks also to Jon Stallworthy and Jane Draycott; Claire Crowther; Anne Berkeley, Sue Leigh, Sue Rose, Siriol Troup and Tamar Yoseloff; Ramez Ghazoul; Helen Richardson; Charles and Wilma; Sudeep Sen; Jason Poore; Dr Irving Finkel and Ros Abramsky; and the translators and editors of my poems into Arabic – especially Adnan al-Sayegh, who has been endlessly patient and kind. Finally, thanks to my cousin, Ann Voss, who helped me rediscover my Welsh roots, and most of all to my sister Gillian Beetham, who gave me invaluable help in tracing our family history and because she has always been by my side.

Some of these poems, or versions of them, have been previously published by or performed at *Ambit*; *Boomslang*; *Molossus*; Pegasus Theatre, Oxford; *Poetry Wales*; *Tellus*; *The Interpreter's House*; *The Oxford Magazine*; *The Oxonian Review*; *World Literature Today*. 'Lunette' was a prize-winner in the Kent and Sussex Competition, judged by Mimi Khalvati. 'Now as Then', 'Song to Inanna/Ishtar' and 'Gilgamesh's Lament' were first published by Mulfran Press in *Now as Then: Mesopotamia-Iraq* (April 2013), a pamphlet of poems in English and Arabic by myself and Adnan al-Sayegh as part of the Arts Council-funded programme of readings and workshops at the Ashmolean Museum to mark the tenth anniversary of the US and UK invasion of Iraq.

As for humans, their days are numbered,
whatever they do is like a puff of wind.

The Epic of Gilgamesh, Tablet III

I think the best thing would be if, at the end of the war we could say we had taken and gained nothing. Taking Mesopotamia, for instance, means spending millions on irrigation and development with no immediate return... keeping up a large army in an unfamiliar country and tackling every kind of tangled administrative question.

Lord Grey of Falloden, *Memories and Reflections*, 1919

Swimmer

for Adnan al-Sayegh

Trust water and it will carry you: after all,
it was our first element: our aqueous cells
cry out to be reunited, go tapping along
inside our skin like blind prisoners, finding

ways back to fluidity: now my hands push
forwards through the gather into a nimbus
of breaking air and I see you move deeper
to a region of mud and reeds, or your fleet

shape harrow sketchy clouds as you break
the wet lid of the river, spray the Euphrates
with falling diamonds. Back then, what you fled
was the midday heat and your father's sickbed –

your mother frayed by the burden of constant
want: later, the soldier's rough, the dirt of spent
cartridges after they'd done their bloody business.
You a poet, darkened by contaminants, restless

with visions, Nimrod's inheritor, buoyed by riffs
of thought as stateless as the fish you swam with.
Now you have another river, feel the pull of other
tides that have brought strangers to the weather

of exile since the Romans. Your voice travels
out, heaped and precious as the Rhondda coals
my father's uncles shovelled, miners like those
who sang to Jesus as Tynewedd waters rose

up the shaft towards them, their wives leaving
spitting kettles to run from their kitchens, drawing
shawls tighter, suddenly old as light pearled:
the pit's last candle drooping like a hanged girl.

Mine

Coal is black diamonds. Every basket is power and civilisation.

Ralph Waldo Emerson

My ancestors worked all day in water, up before dawn, back
after dark – Sunday their only chance at daylight.

The cage and drill hammered their hearts,
the riddling grind of the Widow Maker drove sound
through their bodies into the fault of the mountain.

They walked a mile to the coal face, down branches of air
smelling of clinkers and ponies.

At Rhondda Fawr and Rhondda Fach they mined bitumen
for coke and blacksmiths' fires, laid explosives under buried
forests.

Their hods carried the world's weight,
their bible faces stared down tunnels, their roughness
a chafing in my blood.

Their coal burned harder, hotter, dense seams littered
with dinosaur footprints carried on the flood

from deltas as far away as Umm-Quasir and Basra
to Blaenclydach, where my grandmother, belly taut as a sail,

gasped as her waters
broke and the child in her womb started his journey.

Blaenclydach

A gap like a lost tooth, a space
I can walk across in twenty paces

the house where you were born
now shafts of air, squares of light

where once your father, John,
with wild hair and mother

Myfanwy coupled and clung,
made you with brains enough

to be a doctor and us
respectable.

Later, I stood at their grave
as wind drove rain under the fur

of my anorak hood, watching
the way ivy, tough as coir,

thrust up through the slabs –
its dark leaves

making my own flesh and blood
smell of their bones.

March 1916

Tom

You think of deserts and date palms but this place
floods in spring, temperatures below freezing, sand
turns to bog. Just getting to Qurna was tough going:
everything sank (guns, supplies, men) in a mounting
tide of mud; the injured sloshed along on AT carts,
screaming for morphine. We built a bridge of boats
to reach the so-called Garden of Eden – lanes were
littered with rubbish; in between derelict reed hovels
and dirty gutters we found the Tree of Knowledge –
it was leaning crooked through a shell-pocked roof.

Tom: Second Lieutenant Thomas Charles Lewis

March 2003

Maryam

Suddenly, I saw my son across the square, standing
lost, unprepared under the horizontals of choking
smoke from exploding grenades: I screamed at him
above the jostling crowd but he just stood there,
head bare, brows crouched in a frown. I called again
but my voice fell away; then we were caught in cross-
fire between the Mahdi Army and the Irish Guards –
we realised it was too late to go anywhere. Qurna,
our birthplace, was a conflagration, where Saddam
ruled, Adam and Eve sinned and Alexander died.

Maryam: a Christian Iraqi (interviewed in the *Guardian*, 2009)

Hints for the new recruit 1

1914 – When I Join the Ranks: what to do and how to do it

If you want some advice, don't cling to the company
of untidy soldiers or soldiers of doubtful character;
if you do, you cannot expect officers or anyone else
to have a high opinion of you. Your living quarters

should speak of mathematical precision. Down each
side are arranged the beds, turned up during the day
to form a seat; and overhead is a shelf which contains
portions of your equipment with articles hung from

below on little hooks. It is essential to make sure that
these are kept always tidy and few. Down the centre
you will find plain but well-scrubbed barrack tables
and these last complete the furnishing of the room.

From an MOD pamphlet *Advice to New Recruits*, published 1914
(Imperial War Museum)

Hints for the new recruit 2

When under canvas, life is much the same except
at dawn you'll hear the songs of robin and chaffinch
and see mist rising over distant hills. Now is the time
to practise folding and unfolding your army blanket.

In camp, when weather permits, tent flies should be
rolled up, first thing in the morning: all ground should
be kept scrupulously clean; food should be covered;
empty jam pots should never be allowed to lie about.

You'll find you will never want for company, the sight
of canvas soon brings in the inhabitants of the local
countryside who are only too glad to spend some time
with the lads. If you miss your girl stop reading here.

How Enlil, god of air, sent the Flood to get rid of humans

The Flood terrified everyone, even the gods…
> The Epic of Gilgamesh, The Standard Version, Tablet XI

Enlil hated war. He hated noise pollution and discord.
He warned them in the cities – those that lived in the back
and front streets, those that lived in the shadow of his ziggurat:
but they were unstoppable:

battles, riots, *irshemmas* accompanied by drums, *tigis*
accompanied
by lyres, *adabs* accompanied by … [unidentified instruments]
and worst of all the endless *sir-namsipad-inanna-ka's*
to the shepherdess–goddess Inanna. All this clamour and killing

was unbearable. So Enlil rose up. He shook his fist at the sky
and the rain came down, the Tigris and Euphrates thundered
out of their beds. People fled to higher ground followed by
corpses from the cemetery, floating, with neatly folded hands.

But all were doomed. City and desert slowly turned into ocean.
Enlil cocked an ear to catch any *ireshemmas*, *tigis*, *adabs*
or *sir-namsipad-inanna-ka's* but there were only waves of silence
that went on and on to the edge of the drowned world.

irshemmas, tigis, adabs: types of song
sir-namsipad-inanna-ka's: praises to the shepherdess–goddess Inanna

Hospital barge on the Tigris

In April the desert blooms, even in war:
flowering earlier than a Welsh spring, clustered
along the river bank, rain-scented on a bare, wind-blown
canvas – mallow, shepherd's purse, early-sown
green barley, yellow trefoil and wild mustard,
each day budding with promise of more:

And on the Tigris, a slow hospital ship
carries the wounded, so recently young boys
running home from school down weed-skirted lanes,
now tents of white skin hanging slack on frames
of bone: flies buzz in their mouths, the noise
drowned by the wheel's revolving slap.

April 1916

Tom

Floods three feet deep, often twenty in the old
irrigation ditches. A man accidentally drowned.
The rest, facing the enemy, camped on islands,
Gun Hill, Norfolk Hill, Shrapnel Hill; only reeds,
about two foot high, for a makeshift cover. Each
battalion had sixty bellums to cross the waters.
Five hundred of us British and Indian soldiers
practising punting – a strange regatta! We needed
to find Noah and his ark before we started to go
slowly, one by one and two by two, into the dark.

Strange regatta: this exercise was actually commanded by General
Charles Townshend in 1915 and was known as 'Townshend's
Regatta'.

April 2010

Steve

Reeds are like lungs filtering and cleaning water,
oxygenating the wetlands for hundreds of miles;
their tall stems hide bitterns and slender-billed gulls,
out of their shadows emerge dragonflies, butterflies,
damselflies and the whirligig water beetle; they give
shelter for the Iraq babbler and Basra reed warbler.
The white-eared bulbul and sacred ibis are coming
home to them. Thousands of people make a living
from them. When Saddam cleared them and drained
the marshes people said *Iraq has stopped breathing.*

Steve: Steve Harris, of the Birdscapes Gallery in Holt, Norfolk, who
mounted an exhibition of photographs in 2010 to celebrate the
reflooding of the marshes in Southern Iraq.

Baptism

They could have been made from stone, the same
stone of country houses with walled gardens spurting

valerian: they were freezing, coatless, cold as slate
when marsh water flowed into the trenches carrying

cholera and they went over the top in darkness to meet
darkness lit by enemy flares, stumbling and drowning

with the bolting mules, too numb to know what they
were doing or which way they were supposed to go:

back home the font was wreathed with laurel: it stood
sunlit, under an angel leading a child away from harm.

How the one wise man, Uta-napishtim, survived the Flood

So make yourself an ark of cypress wood;
make rooms in it and coat it with pitch inside and out.

Genesis 6:14

fish flicker in the olive groves, hang like pearls
from the branches of cedars: across space where air
once was, bones float free from skin, electric eels flash
in the eyes of the startled dead

now there is only this, the dark ocean and slick
of whale: a north-east wind brings rain and more rain
until Uta-napishtim's ark clears the mountain top: he sits
with his wives, carving stories

onto clay tablets, remembering how the living were,
the sounds they made, how they crushed mint and lavender
between forefinger and thumb to release the scent:
the tang of honey on the tongue

Anti-tank weapons

Successful for anti-tank weapons, especially when attackers are silhouetted against the sky

Successful for anti-tank weapons, especially short-range man-portable anti-tank rockets. Defiladed positions behind a hill have some important advantages. This is because dead space created by the intervening crest of the hill prevents an approaching tank from using the range of its direct-fire weapons, so that neither the attacker nor defender will have a clear shot until the tank is within range of the camouflaged defending anti-tank weapon when attackers are silhouetted against the sky

The call–up

i.m. Wilfred Owen

A grief ago, spring turned early into ceanothus summer, skies
scoured by keening swifts, and our sons ran out of the pavilion

shining in their whiter-than-white whites, their bats held high:
we waited in the long grass, our shoes drowned in buttercups

as they faced over after over, the onlookers cheering: at least
it wasn't France, we said, its boulevards cobbled with skulls:

there was a pair of goshawks nesting in the wood that year, fierce
birds hooked to the sky like medieval warriors, the female three

times the size of her mate who hardly dared to visit his chicks
with strips of flesh, knowing he came too close on pain of death.

May 1916

Charles

Battalion contrived to build a lunette of sandbags
in a sub-section of the Fortieth. Patrols without
protection, sent out at night and normal sniping
carried on by both sides. Our difficulty with water
supplies was solved by the overnight construction
of two tanks lined with tarpaulins, filled by pakhals
from Abu Roman Mounds (which was a good four
miles away.) They were brought by mules at night
as motor transport failed and not enough mechanics.
Armistice on the third for burial of the Turkish dead.

Charles: Lieutenant Colonel Charles Kitchen, the South Wales
Borderers' war diarist

May 2010

Georgia

I joined on a whim. I think it started as a bet
over a game of pool: loads of big brothers to
look after us girls on nights out, also respect
that you're just one of the lads when it comes
to work. I ran the workshop for broken-down
tanks day and night; there's no time off in war
zones. I was used a lot, as tanks always need a
mechanic on board. You can get killed at any
time. It's hard to explain what fear in people's
faces looks like – even the biggest hardest men.

Georgia: Georgia Watts, mechanic in the British Army on active
service in Basra, 2007 (interviewed 2010)

Lunette

i.

A two- or three-sided field fort,
its rear open to interior lines.

A two- or three-sided field fort
often named in honour of battery
commanders:

(for 'battery' see also 'assault';

see also a collection of multiple
electrochemical cells
or a 'voltaic pile');

even when the frog is dead, its legs will twitch
when touched with electrodes

especially on the dissecting slab with
its rear open to interior lines

ii.

Portion of a vertical plane beneath a semicircular vault
set in an arched opening, possibly a fanlight.

Portion of a vertical plane beneath a semicircular vault
bounded by the intrados and springing-line;

or when a horizontal cornice transects a round-headed arch
at the level of the imposts, where the arch springs:

as in the curve of a back when, in labour, the body arches;

if it's massive and deeply set, it may be called
a tympanum, as in a hearing gland in frogs; or an ear drum –

or a drum-shaped rack on which victims were tortured,
their legs twitching, even when dead, and their souls exiting

a small window
set in an arched opening, possibly a fanlight

iii.

It is used for holding the Host in an upright position
when exposed in the monstrance.

It is used for holding the Host in an upright position
and known in Germany as the *lunula* and also as the *melchisedech*:

it is crescent-shaped, a half-moon clip of gold or silver-gilt
which must be purified when the Host is changed –

pure as moonlight, transparent, an idea of body
that is not flesh, a remonstration, a halving;

the monstrous body made thin enough to slip though
a crack (possibly a fanlight), nerve endings exposed –

bloodless, airless, a rack of ribs
that turns to dust
when exposed in the monstrance

The fall of Kut 1916

Their officers board the boat for Baghdad
leaving them stranded with no superiors:
horses, dogs and cats all killed and eaten,
now the remaining soldiers scrounge
cigarettes and wait, straining their eyes
against the glare, as enemy forces trickle

into Kut. Then the hundred-mile march over
parched land, the gnawing of bull-penis whips,
the bootless, hatless stagger through burning
desert, falling under the two-handed swipe
of the captor's swords, throats stuffed
with sand, heads caved in by rifle butts.

June 1916

Tom

Grass fires fanned by the wind destroyed half our
camp. In under an hour we lost twenty-eight tents;
thieves, taking advantage of the lack of moonlight,
sent out raiding parties to strip anything that was left.
Two deaths from cholera, two from dysentery; fever
is rampant; the horses and mules suffer, like us, from
the curse of flies that swarm in our eyes and mouths;
you swallow scores of them every time you eat: life
here seems arbitrary and cheap. Each time you wake,
touch wood and pray you'll be one of the lucky ones.

June 2010

Adnan

Half my life was spent in wars while the other half
was spent in exile. When war started between Iraq
and Iran in nineteen eighty, the governments took
all the young people for fighting, if not they would
be executed. So we went to war though we didn't
believe in it. Eight years later and we were still there.
One day I was walking, writing poems in my head
when a mule bolted past me: moments later he was
blown to bits, covering me in blood, showing me
how writing and life play together, sewn by chance.

Adnan: Adnan al-Sayegh, an Arabic poet from Iraq, living in exile in
London (interviewed 2010)

Witness statement 1

'...there are a lot of facts in the modern history of Iraq that have not been written in a neutral way. For example, what happened in the revolution of July 14, 1958 in Iraq? Or in the fall of the monarchy and the beginning of the Republic? People in my country have different opinions, some call it a revolution and celebrate it, while others call it a takeover. On the same day, concerts and parties are held by some while others mourn. Yet I believe that war is often or always bad. From my studies about the history of my country and the region's history, and from having lived through three wars in Iraq, wars always inherit blood. It is true that the recent war saved us from dictatorship but it brought us another war, destruction, murders, bombings, political and religious conflicts and economic downfall. It added more wounds. Despite all that, I do sometimes feel optimistic because I believe that freedom is always more beautiful. I still change my thoughts and mood about what happened after April 9, 2003, and many people in Iraq share my uncertainty.'

from an interview with Adnan al-Sayegh, July 2010

Gilgamesh dreams of Enkidu in the wilderness

He of the steppe shall come and chase out the one from the city
Old Babylonian liver omen

In a mountainous and wooded country
with his doe-eyed favourite he's far
from the High Priest treading the
thousand steps: far from the incantations

of the temple choir at Eanna, the harp
found in the death pit of the Royal Cemetery,
the bearded bull of solid gold at Ur,
the headdress of lapis lazuli and cornelian,

the woman made of squares, the scarab-swaddled
baby: he places his hand on her flank, her vellum
hide hiding a shop of tales: on the stele they press on
up towards the great breast of the sun.

Enkidu: his name translates as 'Lord of Pleasant Places' – or 'Wild
Nature'
Eanna: the main temple of Uruk

July 1916

Tom

Temperatures of one hundred and twenty-five
degrees Fahrenheit. Little relief, heat made even
worse by dust storms and high winds blowing
the grit in our eyes so we must screw them up
to avoid being blinded. When Kut fell in April,
our generals trembled as Baghdad grew strong;
now we have to take back their cities from them –
cities that seem so alien yet familiar. We can still
trace our beliefs back here, where our own God
roared from the burning bush *thou shalt not kill*.

July 2009

Peter

The Iraqi capital, as we generals often like to say,
is the centre of gravity for the larger mission in
Iraq. If Baghdad goes under with sectarian strife,
the cause of fostering a more stable Iraq is lost.
But if, as we wish, the position can be improved,
we hope the effects will finally be felt elsewhere.
In invading Iraq, American forces started from
outside the country and fought their way into it.
The current strategy is essentially to work from
the inside outwards – as *Baghdad goes, so goes Iraq*.

Peter: Lieutenant General Peter W. Chiarelli, Vice Chief of Staff of
the US Army Multi-National Corps – Iraq, 1st Cavalry Division

Non-military statements

1. Neutralisation [*killing soldiers*] is part of any war
   as are soft targets [*bombing civilians*].

2. Life deprivation [*killing anyone*] and surgical strikes
   [*shelling and bombing*] can be justified.

3. Extraordinary rendition [*kidnapping*] of illegal combatants
   [*people we don't like*] is necessary in the war against terror.

4. Enhanced coercive interrogation [*torture*] is used to get the
   truth about weapons of mass destruction [*biological,
   chemical, nuclear and imaginary*].

5. Collateral damage [*civilian deaths*] is unfortunate as is the
   number of non-viable combat personnel [*wounded soldiers*].

6. The number of incidents of friendly fire [*accidentally killed by
   own troops*] is regrettable as is the body count of non-opera-
   tives [*dead soldiers*].

7. During war, more money can often be generated through
   sales of weapons than in times of permanent pre-hostility
   [*peace*].

Gilgamesh and Enkidu seek fame by killing the giant Humbaba

I'll make a name for myself that will last for ever!

The Epic of Gilgamesh, Tablet II

A path through the trees, well trodden, bladed
with axe-light: Humbaba's seven radiant auras
slip away: the evening sky turns sulphurous
over Babylon; at the New Moon festival

the High Priest holds up the cup of gold
to the half-year god, and Enkidu, remembering
his dream, senses the stink of death on him,
hears Humbaba's blood cry out from the ground.

Gilgamesh's hand on his shoulder, once friendly,
now carries a burden of war and plague
to be dragged to the end: a hind's eye hidden
among familiar leaves catches the last rays.

August 1916

Tom

The land and sky trick us with mirages of enemy
troops becoming trestle tables which float over
the ground towards us before turning into camels
and disappearing into thin air. We can't tell how
many or how close they are – we dive for cover,
frightened by bushes: sunset behind a mound
is the flare of shrapnel over shepherds watching
their flocks under the stars. These are the rocks
where Cain heard God's voice sound, saying –
your brother's blood cries out to me from the ground!

August 2006

Hamid

Basra, ancient city of parks smelling of flowers
and spices, renowned place of coffee-houses,
mosques and the intricate façades of buildings
of old Ashar: everywhere water mirrors sky –
kingfishers and bee-eaters dart in the shadows
of date palms. Sinbad's city is now populated
by children, all the young men dead in the wars.
Hamid, beautiful child, rises at dawn to collect
scrap metal, building a new life from Pepsi cans:
he says – *peace is the greatest treasure we could ask for.*

According to the *Observer* (2009) more than half the 1.5 million
residents of Basra are children.

Father

My face is made from yours —
your jaw, your weak right eye:
my shin bone's from your leg,
shattered in the moonlight
as you supervised the digging
of the trench at Kut-al-Amara.

Years on, your long-dead smile
watched us from walls, sideboards:
from our mother's dressing table
casting a shadow round her heart
like your shadow in the album
as you pointed the Box Brownie

towards the Bridge of Boats
at Qurna, the army camp at Kut:
Father, those splinters of bone
were your salvation, hard shards
from which I sprang with shared
ancestry, looking for you.

Second Lieutenant T.C. Lewis

Bridge of boats at Qurna

Basra

Arab merchants on the Tigris

Bartering on the banks of the Tigris

Bridge of boats at Sheikh Saad

Laying in stores, Sheikh Saad

Song for Inanna/Ishtar

Your eyes, the twin rivers
Tigris and Euphrates
two great flocks winding through the night
mirrored by star-fields.

Capriciously, you dispose of your lovers –
the gardener, the water-carrier, the leopard-headed king.
You indulged him a full year until he was led
uncomplaining to the edge of the furrow.

Your breath smells of hooves and spit.
Your body emits the shimmer of bulls.
The grain of your groin is horned and cloven.
When you open your legs
your vastness swallows us whole.

September 1916

Tom

Shûmal has dropped, now only ninety-two degrees
in the shade. For the past twenty-four hours we've
had an armistice for exchange of prisoners. Over
fifty men to hospital, one shot his own finger off.
The rest began the ninety-mile march to Amara,
some following by boat. Dust so thick we can't
see our hands. We set off before dawn to avoid
the heat and often cover over fifteen miles a day.
Abu Bishot, Hansalayan, Abu Shitaib; if this next
push is successful, we'll set our sights on Baghdad.

September 2010

Ramez

My childhood in Iraq was idyllic. Unlike today's children in Iraq, we had complete security and there was no war affecting our daily life. World War Two was raging at the time, but it was far away from us, so we children were hardly aware of it, which is such a difference from children in Iraq now living under the occupation. When I was studying in Baghdad I started to become aware of a wider world where injustice and wars were actually the norm, rather than the exception.

Ramez: Ramez Ghazoul, an Iraqi Christian from Mosul living in exile (interviewed 2010)

Witness statement 2

'...as a direct consequence of America's and Britain's war and occupation of Iraq, over one million people have been killed, five million people have been displaced or become refugees, and nearly all Iraqi children have been traumatised – either physically or psychologically. The Anglo-American occupation of Iraq has fuelled ethnic and sectarian strife. The so-called elections have been conducted on the basis of sectarian demarcations. Such elections under occupation are similar to the election of the Vichy regime in France under Nazi occupation, and are no more valid. I'm afraid history will perceive Tony Blair's egoistic policies as a badge of shame on the British people. The removal of Saddam Hussein from power has to be viewed as positive. But this begs the question: at what cost? Can anyone honestly balance this outcome against the horrendous suffering inflicted on millions of Iraqis?'

Interview with Ramez Ghazoul, July 2010

Notes from exile

for Ramez Ghazoul

i. Cucumbers

in this Garden of Eden where Genghis
and Alexander left their marks and Cain
murdered Abel: in this garden, this same
garden, I tended my little patch of soil
growing melons with their showy yellow
trumpets, and cucumbers, water-holders,
tubes of coolness shining in the desert
before the Flood, before the King List:
known to Kurds, Arabs and Turkomans,
Muslims, Christians, Jews and Chaldeans,
Armenians, Yezidis, atheists: children
of Mesopotamia who might have run
at first light to cut the best one, saying,
as I did – *father, I've grown this for you.*

ii. Umm-Ulrabiain

in Mosul, when the hottest hours
made work and studying unbearable,
we slept on thin blankets in the large
hall, its porous marble surface sprayed
with water, as outside, in our copious
garden, birds fled to the veined shade
of pistachio trees to escape the sun
that scorched the lawns we played on,
made too hot to touch the taps that
hung with icicles in winter; it mellowed
only in the spring and autumn seasons
when my family picnicked in the fields
outside our city which is often called
Umm-Ulrabiain, or *Mother of Two Springs*.

iii. Occupation

a gap in the stones, a bowl of air and sky
stippled like trout skin, barred by cloud
like a pheasant's wing: that airiness
flew inside us, that safety and freedom
roamed the archaeological ruins of cities
with us — Khorsabad, Hatra and Nimrood —
while bees on the purple thistle were like
jewels on a pincushion, and butterflies
darting, stitching green fretworks, sipped
moisture from the muddy track we trod
until, at the end of the day, we trekked
home to bed, leaving behind the ravaged
past and the buzzard above us, sky-hunter,
wind-driven ahead of the carnage to come.

October 1916

Tom

Two lots of mail from home with some letters
for me, at last, giving news from Glamorgan.
Mother unwell for the past few weeks, although
she puts on a brave face as usual. Sister Betty is
still on her drive to collect wool for the knitting
of balaclavas: I said *they'll be back to front no doubt!*
Here we are stuck in the desert while their lives
keep on almost as usual there in dear old Wales
except it's now a place where there are no young
men and people tell each other *no news is good news.*

October 2009

Mahdi

My father now lives in exile and I write to him
that our football games are played beside swamps
of sewage and toxic waste. The electricity supply
cuts out all the time making our computers crash:
yet things in Basra are better than they used to be.
My dream is for stability here to continue, for poor
people to live with dignity. I want to get married –
provide for myself and my family. Basra floats on
oil; if it falls into honest hands it will be good news:
we can lift Basra up and my father will come back.

Mahdi: Mahdi Abdullah, aged 15, a Muslim boy (interviewed in
the *Observer*, 2009)
Basra floats on oil: Iraq possesses some 113 billion gallons of oil
reserves, making it the second largest known oil supply in the
world, following Saudi Arabia. Iraq is almost literally floating on
an underground sea of oil.

Mother

Childbirth was like being excavated:
my belly rose on whalebone wings,
pain soared about me like a bloodied angel:

then you were born

I saw you with my own eyes
I held you day and night:
you lay in my arms, a glowing pupa.

At Kut-al-Amara you were back-lit,
the moon pointed you out against the ridge —
when Turkish gunners stopped your spade

you fell slowly, shedding iridescence

each night in dreams I fail to catch you —
your bones the fragile quills of rescued fledglings
you placed by the stove for warmth

The gods punish Gilgamesh with Enkidu's death

To those left behind, the gods give heartache.

The Epic of Gilgamesh, Tablet VII

When I laid my hand on your shoulder, you turned to me.
When you turned to me, I saw you weren't smiling.
When I saw you weren't smiling, I knew the gods would
punish us.
When I knew the gods would punish us, I tried to placate them.
When I tried to placate them, they closed their minds to me.
When they closed their minds to me, I knew it was hopeless.
When I knew it was hopeless, I cut my chest with a knife.
When I cut my chest with a knife, the blood spurted out.
When the blood spurted out, a maggot fell from your nostril.
When a maggot fell from your nostril, I had to leave your body.
When I had to leave your body, I wandered in the wilderness.
When I wandered in the wilderness, I dreamed about you.
When I dreamed about you, I laid my hand on your shoulder.
When I laid my hand on your shoulder, you turned to me.
When you turned to me, I saw you weren't smiling.

The Regimental Collect of the Royal Regiment of Wales

Dragwyddol Dduw, ein Tad nefol, a roddaist dy Fab Jesu Grist i farw drosom a'i godi o'r meirw; erfyniwn arnat gynnal gwroldeb hynafol y Cmry Brenhinol, fel y gallwyn bob amser ddilyn llwybr dyletswydd yn ô lei Esiampl a thrwy Ei ras fod yn deilwng o'th Deyrnas dragwyddol; drwy'r un Jesu Grist ein Harglwydd. Amen.

Eternal God, our heavenly Father, who gave your son Jesus Christ to die for us and raised him up from the dead; uphold, we pray, the ancient valour of the Royal Welsh, that we may follow the path of duty after His example and by His grace be found worthy of your eternal Kingdom; through the same Jesus Christ our Lord. Amen.

Gilgamesh seeks the wise man Uta-napishtim

Wherever I look, I see death,
wherever I turn, death is beside me.

The Epic of Gilgamesh, Tablet XI

The *gidim xul* and *maskim xul*, ghosts
that ambush from the silt of dreams,
each night cause Enkidu to rise unsmiling
in a desert of stone moons:

Gilgamesh dogged by demons urges boatman
Ur-shanabi to pilot him across the waters
to where Uta-napishtim sits eating honey
contemplating eternity: each thought lasts

a lifetime, each lifetime another lifetime: scents
of mint and lavender – defeating sleep impossible,
let alone death: but Gilgamesh pleads for release
from death. He wants eternal life.

gidim xul: evil ghost
maskim xul: demon who lies in wait

November 1916

Tom

No sun but a brightness of cloud with light
coming in straight rays which cast a diffused
shine over the roads and turn them to silver.
Shell craters full of water, like pot holes of a
Welsh lane, frustrate movement of men, guns
and mules: it's almost beautiful, yet moments
later, we are shelling a village with women and
children on fire, running for their lives. I weep.
Christ said *suffer the little children to come to me*
yet how we make those little children suffer.

November 2009

Khwater

My name is Khwater Sadeq, when the war came
we had terrible suffering, shelling from the air,
explosions, tanks, suicide bombers: all the time
fear for me and my seven sisters: after our mum
and dad were killed by US bombs we came to the
al-Zahara Organisation for Orphans: and now I
try to throw my mind forward to school lessons,
the joys of music and religious songs: to a future
where I can walk to and from school in safety;
where I can follow my computer studies in peace.

Khwater: Khwater Sadeq, aged 13, a Muslim orphan (interviewed in
the *Guardian*, 2009)

is now as then, a landscape   as far as the eye can see over
barren mountains and stony   mule tracks winding through
deserts, fields of barley, palm   trees bearing dates: reed beds,
tremulous openings to fields   frequented by the Iraq babbler
and Basra reed warbler: now   the sacred ibis is coming home
to a past still alive, alluvium   creating fertile plains: air can't
remember snow as ours does   that fine hint of chill on new
March mornings round papery   narcissi, daffodils, crocuses
blue hyacinths: here, at Shatt al Arab, Tigris and Euphrates
meet (stealth bombers and cruise missiles arc across the
desert sky. American and British TV news describe
it as the 'terrible beauty' of war.) And now we
have the siege of Basra: million and a half
people, forty per cent of them children.
No clean water or food. Control of the
waterway and its uses as a border have
been a source of contention between
predecessors of the Iranian and Iraqi
states since a peace treaty in sixteen
thirty-nine which divided the territo
ry according to old customs withou
t relying on a survey. The tribes on
both sides of the lower waterway ar
e Marsh Arabs whom the Ottoman
s claimed to represent, but tension
between the opposing empire exte
nded across conflicts leading to out
breaks of hostilities in the nineteen
th century which resulted in the Se
cond Treaty of Erzurum between t
sa raf sa si won sa neht a epacsdnal
halb halb…halb

halb…

Siduri the tavern keeper advises Gilgamesh

I can look you in the eye, Tavern Keeper,
but I can't face death.

The Epic of Gilgamesh, Sippar Tablet

Gilgamesh, what's wrong with you?
You'll never find what you're looking for:
when the gods gave humans life
they also gave them death.
They kept eternity for themselves.

For this is human destiny.

But you, Gilgamesh, eat! Drink!
Enjoy yourself! Put on your best clothes,
wash your hair, have a relaxing bath!
Make the most of what's precious to you —
your child's hand in yours,
the arms of your loving wife.

For this too is human destiny.

December 1916

Tom

We pushed on from Sheikh Saad to Kut: mud
made going hard, then on again to Atab ford
in freezing weather: dumped all our blankets
except one each: at Imam-al-Mansur, we left
the tents and carts, line was a series of redans
on a three-mile front five hundred yards apart.
About to leave when suddenly, Turkish guns
fired on us, killing one man: then heavy shelling
killed Second Lieutenant Gould plus four more.
Families have been told they died with courage.

December 2006

Sarah

I listen for his voice in the wind on the hillside:
this is where he used to play as a child. All that
love he grew up with carried as a shield, proved
no match for this oilfield war with its roadside
bombs far from Glyndwr's *teulu* and the bracken
tombs of wandering Irish saints bringing Christ
to Cardiff. They call him a Welsh warrior, say that
he died with glory, laid down his life so that others
could be saved: it was cold when he died, they said –
a stray bullet just as they were packing up to leave.

Sarah: Sarah Jones, mother of a soldier killed in Iraq (poem inspired
by BBC news report, 2010)

The Welsh Horse

The wind of heaven is that which blows between a horse's ears.

Arab proverb

There's slate in his flanks, reflecting sea and sky:
his face, slate-coloured, split by a zig-zag flash
of white, as he nuzzles the hands of children
for sugar, trots out with the greys and the reds:
how the heart swells to the sound of a band!
Between his ears blows the wind of heaven.

There's slate on the beaches of a Welsh haven
slate in the rain and the pebble-dashed sky,
slate in the eyes of the Bethesda band
trotting out 'Men of Harlech' with the same flash
of pride Mohammed felt as his white, pure-bred
mare guzzled the fleeting wind: and here, children

get a breath of the sirocco, these children
who still believe that God in His heaven
blesses only their own fathers in the red
uniforms of The Welsh Horse as, under skies
layered with shale and cloud, they go flashing
past making the earth sing as the marching band

plays 'The British Grenadiers', and the band-
leader on his shire horse delights the children
with 'Warriors of Glamorgan', glints flashing
off his kettle drums under a Welsh heaven
not far from the horse's own patch of sky
tethered to the headland under the reds

and ambers of a quiet sunrise: as red
poppies explode across the fields like bands
of rubies catching fire from Arab skies
over the desert's scattered bones – and children
left fatherless in a deserted heaven,
now feel their own lives rush past in a flash –

their fathers' ghosts, like the intermittent flash,
through cloud, of low-flying bombers on red
alert, fade with each slow pulse until heaven
becomes no more than a trace, like the bands
of sea thrift along tracks taken by children
to visit the old horse, framed by evening sky:

now he hardly remembers how the sky flashed
with children: the cavalry officers' red
coats or the band's airs which were once his heaven.

Hints for the new recruit 3

On how to properly address superiors, see page two
section two of *Compliments paid by Guards and Sentries*
(price two pence). Other forms of address may confuse
but you'll soon pick up the lingo and become fluent

in slinging the bat: whether you're a sapper, a one pip
or a loot you'll be scoffing the same grub and necking
the same grog as the next soldier. If you get in a funk
about going west when you get the order to go up –

reach for a gasper to calm your nerves, no-one likes
having to jump the bags, wait for the plum puddings
to drop or go to the shooting gallery: but take heart,
not everyone ends up a landowner in the rest camp.

Slinging the bat: using army slang

Hints for the new recruit 4

It's not that hard to get yourself a soup ticket or even
a rooti gong, specially in Mesopalonica fighting Johnny.
If you have to join the suicide club, take precautions
such as making pretty sure you're never the third man –

that's a sure way to get pipped and you'll find yourself
pushing up the daisies toot sweet. Get yourself a Blighty
One and you'll be in velvet. Better to be on the peg than
on the wire, although both best avoided. If you're a base

wallah, get busy with the bluebell and blanco, send off
a few quick firers and if it's Thursday, get ready for a Poets
but make sure you keep your tin opener in good order
or you risk an early visit to the stiff's smoked haddock.

The third man: a reference to soldiers lighting cigarettes. The enemy
was alerted by the first light, took aim at the second and fired at the
third.
Poets: Friday, i.e. 'Push Off Early, Tomorrow's Saturday'

January 1917

Charles

Kut-al-Amara, night of the eleventh, at one a.m. –
brilliant moon showed men on covering duty
for trench-digging. Second Lieutenant Lewis
and seven men were wounded by enemy fire.
Second Lieutenant Evans killed. On fifteenth,
Major Fairweather killed, also four others killed
and two wounded. Has to be one of our worst
months yet in this campaign. Hail, rain and mud:
the enemy flood the trenches with cholera-filled
marsh water; we go hungry, no sign of rations.

January 2009

Jason

It was two thousand and four – I joined up with Heavy Equipment – pretty exciting, I was only twenty. Kut-al-Amara was a shit-hole, I was there to build and repair observation posts and roads – just a back-up role, it wasn't too bad, but this time round, I feel shitty, I don't wanna go back. I'll be doing the most dangerous job there is, clearing routes, tracking IEDs, with grenade launchers that jam, rifles that don't fire. My mate got lucky, sent home with a leg wound. Grandma says I'm brave.

Jason: Jason Poore, a US Marine (interviewed in 2009)

Wound shock

at Kut-al-Amara he was back-lit

He suffered many and grievous hurts.

the moon pointed him out against the ridge

The Thomas knee-splint was used in gunshot fracture-
wounds of the femur.

when British soldiers stopped his spade

No-one knew what happened to the lost blood, no single
aetiological factor has been suggested.

he fell slowly, shedding iridescence

A marked disturbance of the normal mechanisms of blood is
usual.

each night in dreams she fails to catch him

The historian finds himself confronted with a volume of
clinical observations.

his bones the fragile quills

The collapse that accompanies severe wounding and loss of
blood has been studied by military surgeons as far back as
Hippocrates.

of rescued fledglings he placed by the stove for warmth

The wise man Uta-napishtim advises Gilgamesh

You're wearing yourself out with all this stress.

The Epic of Gilgamesh, Tablet X

Gilgamesh, you're headed for an early grave,
you're riddled with discontent
yet your life could end at any moment –
cut off like a reed in the reed bed.

The gorgeous young man, the lovely girl –
in a flash, death could hack them down:
yet we go on grabbing as much as we can, feathering
our own nests, squabbling over money, starting wars:

      while all the time, the river
rises and floods, the mayfly skims the water,
the sun blazes down on us each day, until all of a sudden –
      it's over!

Learning to love my high heel leg

Losing my leg was the worst thing,
I couldn't even bath my daughter,
my husband has got me through,
now I can wear Manolo Blahniks.

I couldn't even bath my daughter,
I've got to get my weight down
now I can wear Manolo Blahniks,
I've started running for the first time.

I've got to get my weight down,
I'm going to be running for charity,
I've started running for the first time
to help limbless soldiers like myself.

I'm going to be running for charity,
it's hard but I have to keep trying
to help limbless soldiers like myself.
I feel now the leg is a part of me.

It's hard but I have to keep trying,
my husband has got me through,
I feel now the leg is a part of me,
though losing it was the worst thing.

Corporal Hannah Campbell lost her leg in an Iraqi mortar attack.
Eighteen months later (April 2012) she ran the London Marathon
with a prosthetic leg.

No other heaven pleased me

Sometimes I stroke my own hair, imagining
my father's hand laid against the contours
of the warm earth or palm up towards the sun

cupping a hazelnut smooth as a face, its flesh
safe inside its shell until I break it open to find
nothing; the distances have been too great

across broken, unreconnoitred ground; pushing
forward and falling back, going over and over
the same stretch searching for a river, a riverbed,

tracks of a railway or even a mule, anything
that's been that way before instead of just
names in war diaries – Beit Aisa, Deli Abbas,

Falujah – all far away and hard to get to with
only the moon as compass, bent at her sculling
as space between us stiffens and cools.

Now as then

Read our footprints on the long road out of Babylon.
They'll tell you

how the river stopped and fish became tin; how the air
had a taste of marble and our lungs fought for breath
as they turned to stone –

how our selves disappeared
into the shadows of date palms cast in bronze
on the walls of Sennacherib's palace.

Still we journey, unembraceable ghosts,
flying across continents between airports, each new city a
                                                    sarcophagus
from which the winged genies who protect us have fled.

And always the scent of cedar and cypress, boxwood and
                                                    juniper.
Always the mayfly hovering over the water.
Always the mother and child leaving their country for ever.

Epilogue

...whatever they do is like a puff of wind...

what wound into the canals was music, snaking
into the wounds of war, the desert's music
of water, irrigating and cleansing: war's music

is a bombardment of timpani and bugle sounds –
thin drifts of smoke winding into the sky above
dunes and trenches above humans and animals

roaring for an end: a few birds, the slap of clothes
being washed on stones, the lap of the bloodied
river in the reeds, but by evening, shepherd's pipes

goat bells and crickets: sounds of life trying
to go on as long as water continues to flow

السبّاح
Swimmer

ترجمة: غسان نامق
مراجعة: د. صلاح نيازي

إلى عدنان الصائغ

ضَعْ ثقتَكَ بالماء وهو سيَحمِلُك: ففي نهاية المطافِ،
هو عُنصرُنا الأولُ: وخلايانا المائيةُ
تصرُخُ ليلتئمَ شَمْلُها، تَدُقُّ
على جدارِ جِلدِنا مثل سُجناءَ عُميان، فتَجِدُ

سُبُلاً للعودةِ إلى السيولةِ: والآن تندفعُ يداي
خلالَ الجَمْعِ إلى هالةِ
هواءٍ مُتَكَسِّرٍ، فأراكَ تتغلغلُ
في منطقةِ طينٍ وقَصَبٍ، أو أرى

هيئتَكَ المُسْرِعةَ تَسحو سحاباً ضئيلاً وأنت تَكسِرُ
الغِطاءَ النديَّ للنهرِ وتنثُرُ على الفراتِ
ماساً متساقطاً. وهناك، ما هَرَبتَ منه
هو حرارةُ مُنتصفِ النهار وسريرُ مَرَضٍ والدِكَ —

ووالدتُكَ التي أنهَكَها العِبءُ الدائمُ:
وبَعدَ ذلك، خشونةُ الجنديةِ، وقذارةُ الخراطيشِ المُستهلَكةِ
بَعدَ أدائها عملَها الدمويَّ.
وأنتَ الشاعرُ الذي أحزَنتْكَ المُرَبياتُ، وأقلقتْكَ

مع الأخيلةِ، يا وريثَ النمرودِ، طَفوتَ بمقطوعاتِ
أفكارٍ لا وطنَ لها، كما السمكةُ التي سبحتَ معها.
والآن لديكَ نهرٌ آخر وتحسُّ بجَذبٍ آخر للمَدِّ والجَزْر
جَلَبَ غُرَباءَ إلى طقسٍ

المنفى، منذ الرومان. وصوتُك يَرتحلُ،
مُتراكماً وثميناً مثلَ فحم روْنذا*
الذي جَرَفَهُ أعمامُ أبي، عُمّالُ مناجمَ كأولئك الذينَ
أنشدوا للمسيحِ حين صَعَدَتْ مياهُ تِيْنيويد**

إليهم عبر المَهوى، فتَرَكَتْ زوجاتُهم
غَلّاياتِهِن الفائرةَ لِيَهرُبْنَ من مَطابخِهِنّ، وأحكمنَ
رَبْطَ شالاتِهِنَّ، وهرِمنَ فجأةً مع تشظّي النورِ:
شمعةُ المنْجَمِ الأخيرةِ تَهدلّتْ مثل فتاةٍ مشنوقة.

هوامش المترجم:

* "روْنذا": قصبة تقع عند "نهر روْندا" في جنوب "ويلز". ويشار إليها باسم "وادي روْندا" الذي يتكون
من واديين اثنين لاستخراج الفحم.

** "تِيْنيويد": قرية واقعة في "قصبة روْندا" في جنوب "ويلز" وفيها منجم فحم.

المَنْجَم
Mine

ترجمة: غسان نامق
مراجعة: ع. الصائغ

"الفحمُ؛ ماسٌ أسود. كُلُّ سلعةٍ، طاقةٌ وحَضارةٌ."
– رالف والدو إميرسون –

أسلافي كانوا يعملونَ طوالَ اليوم في الماءِ، يذهبونَ في البزوغِ، ويعودون
بعدَ انسدالِ الظلام — والأحدُ؛ فرصتُهمُ الوحيدةُ لرؤيةِ ضوءِ النهار.

القَفَصُ والمِثقابُ يَطرُقان أفئِدتَهم،
واهتزازُ الطاحونةِ* المتعاقبُ يدفعُ الصوتَ
عبرَ أجسادِهم إلى صَدعِ الجبلِ.

يَسيرونَ ميلاً نحوَ وَجهِ الفحمِ، ويهبطونَ في فروعٍ من الهواء
تَفوحُ منها رائحةُ المعادنِ المصهورةِ والمُهَراةِ

في روندا فاور وروندا فاخ** يَستخرجونَ القارَ
للكوكِ ونارِ الحدّادين، ويَضَعونَ المتفجّراتِ
تحتَ الأحراجِ المدفونة.

دِلاءُ فحمِهم تَحمِلُ وزنَ العالمِ،
ووجوهُهمُ الإنجيليةُ تُحملِقُ في الأنفاقِ، وخُشونتُهم
تمورُ في دمي.

كان فحمُهم أشَدَّ وأسخَنَ اشتعالاً، والعروقُ الكثيفةُ مَلأى
بآثارِ أقدامِ ديناصوراتٍ حَمَلَها الطوفان

مِن دلتاتٍ بعيدةٍ، بُعدَ أم قصر والبصرة
إلى بلاينكليداخ*** حيثُ جَدَّتي، بَطْنِها المشدودِ مِثلَ شِراعٍ،

شَهِقَتْ حينَ اندفعَتْ مياهُها****
والطفلُ في رَحِمِها بدأ رحلتَه

هوامش المترجم:

- رالف والدو إميرسون: فيلسوف وشاعر وكاتب أمريكي،(1803-1882).

* وردت بالنص الإنجليزي كلمة Widow Maker وترجمتها الحرفية هي (صانع الأرامل)، إشارةً إلى أن العمل بهذه الآلة في المناجم يؤدي إلى خسارة في الأرواح. وأثناء ترجمتي القصيدة، إحترثُ بهذه التسمية، فبحثت عنها في مختلف المصادر من قواميس وسوى ذلك، ووجدتُ أن عمال المناجم يطلقون تسميات على مثقاب الحفر وذلك حسب المناطق، بحيث صار من الممكن التعرّف على منطقة المناجم من خلال التسمية التي يطلقها العمال على تلك الآلة.

** "رونلا فاور"، و "رونلا فاخ": الواديان اللذان يتكون منهما "وادي رونلا" في جنوب "ويلز".

*** "بلاينكليداخ": قرية واقعة في "قصبة رونلا" ضمن "وادي رونلا" في جنوب "ويلز".

**** سائلها الأمنيوسي.

83

أغسطس 1916، توم
August 1916, Tom

ترجمة: د. بهاء عبد المجيد

مراجعة: ع. الصائغ

الأرضُ والسماءُ؛ تخدعُنا بسرابِ أعداءٍ

قواتُهم أصبحتْ ركائزَ طاولاتٍ، تنتشرُ في الأرضِ باتجاهِنا

قبلَ أن تتحولَ إلى إبلٍ وتختفي في الهواءِ

لا نستطيعُ أن نخمّنَ ما عددهم، أو مدى اقترابِهم

ولكننا نغوصُ لنتخفى،

خائفين من الأدغالِ:

غروب الشمسِ خلف رابيةٍ؛ هو لمعٌ من شظايا

فوق الرعاةِ، تريهم قطعانَهم تحت النجومِ

هذه هي الصخورُ، حيث سمعَ قابيلُ صوتَ الربِّ قائلاً:

- دمُ أخيكَ يستصرخُ بي من الأرضِ!

أغسطس 2006، حميد
August 2006, Hamid

ترجمة: د. بهاء عبد المجيد
مراجعة: ع. الصائغ

يا بصرة؛ يا مدينةٌ قديمةٌ من حدائقَ تعبقُ بالزهورِ
والتوابلَ، ومقاهي القهوةِ الشهيرةِ،
والمساجد بأبنيتها ذات الواجهاتِ المعقودةِ،
في العشّار القديمِ: حيثُ في كلِّ بقعةٍ، يعكسُ النهرُ السماءَ –
وطيورَ الرفرافِ، والوروارية آكلةُ النحلِ، تنطلقُ بخفةٍ، في ظلالِ أشجارِ النخيلِ.
يا مدينةَ السندبادِ، مزدحمةٌ أنتِ الآنَ بالأطفالِ*
لأنَّ الكثيرَ من الشبابِ ماتوا في الحروبِ.
والطفل الجميل حميد، يستيقظُ فجراً ليجمعَ بقايا الصفيح
ليبني بيتاً جديداً من علبِ البيبسي كولا
ومع ذلك يقولُ أن السلامَ هو أثمنُ كنزٍ يمكننا طلبه.

---

* 1.5 مليون هم سكان البصرة، أكثر من نصفهم هم من الأطفال (الراصد 2009).

85

أبي
Father

ترجمة: أحمد الحمدي
مراجعة: ع. الصائغ

وجهي تشكّلَ من وجهكَ –
فكُّكَ والعينُ اليمنى الواهنةُ:
عَظْمةُ قصبتي من ساقِك،
وقد تشظّتْ تحتَ ضوءِ القمر
حيثُ أشرفتَ على حَفْرِ
خندقِ الكوت – العمارة.

بعد سنينٍ؛ وابتسامتُكَ المديدةُ الخامدةُ
ما زالتْ تطالعنا من الجدران، من أخاوينَ:
من طاولةِ زينةِ أمِنا
ملقيةً ظلاً حول قلبِها
شبيبة ظلِكَ في الألبوم
وأنت تشيرُ إلى الكاميرا

باتجاهِ الجسرِ العائمِ على القوارب
في القرنةِ، وعند معسكرِ الجيشِ في الكوت:
أبي؛ تلك شظايا عظامِك
كانت خلاصَكَ، كسراتٌ صلبةٌ
منها أنا نشأتُ،
مع أسلافٍ شاركوني
وأنا أبحثُ عنكَ.

أغنية إلى اينانا / عشتار
Song for Inanna/Ishtar

ترجمة: د. تاج السر كندورة
مراجعة: ع. الصائغ

عيناكِ؛ النهرانِ التوأمانِ
دجلة والفراتُ
هما سربانِ عظيمانِ، يلتفان خللَ الليل
يعكسان حقلاً من النجومِ.

بنزوةٍ؛ تركلين عشاقَك:
البستانيَّ، والسَّقَّاءَ، والملكَ الذي له رأسُ فهدٍ،
غَمَستِه بالملذاتِ، لعام كامل، حتى تمَّ اقتيادُهُ
إلى حافةِ اللحدِ، دونَ أن يشِّكو.

لأنفاسكِ رائحةُ حوافرَ وبصاقٍ
جسدُكِ ينفثُ وميضَ الثيران
وملتقى فخذيكِ مصدرٌ للطاقةِ والإغواء
وعندما تفتحين ساقيكِ
فإن اتساعَكِ يزدردُنا جميعاً.

مُلاحظاتٌ من المَنفى
Notes from exile

ترجمة: غسان نامق
مراجعة: ع. الصائغ

إلى رامز غزول

1. قِثَّاء

في جَنّة عَدن هذه حيث جنكيز
والإسكندر تركا أثرَهما، وحيث قابيل
قتل هابيل: في تلك الجنة، تلك
الجنة ذاتِها، إعتنيتُ بتربة أرضي الصغيرة
فزرعتُها بالشمّامِ ذي الأزهارِ الصفراء المبهرة
بوقيّةِ الشكلِ، وبالقِثَّاءِ الذي يَحتجزُ الماءَ،
أنابيبُ بُرودةٍ تلتمعُ في الصحراء
قَبلَ الطوفان وقَبلَ قائمة الملوكِ:
عرفه الأكراد والعرب والتركمان
والمسلمون والمسيحيون واليهود والكلدانيون
والأرمن والإيزيديون والملحدون: أبناءُ
بلادِ ما بين النهرين الذين ربما انطلقوا
مع الضياء الأول لقَطْفِ أفضَلِه وهم يقولون،
مثلما كنتُ أقولُ: أبتاه؛ زَرَعتُ هذا، لك

2. أمُّ الرَّبيعَين

في المَوصِل، حيث أكثرُ الساعاتِ سُخونة
تَجعلُ العملَ والدراسةَ لا يُحتملان،
كنا نَرقُدُ على بطانياتٍ خفيفةٍ في القاعة
الكبيرة، أرضيَّتُها الرخاميةُ المساميةُ مرشوشةٌ
بالماء، بينما في الخارج، في حديقتنا
المكتظِّةٍ، تفرُّ الطيورُ إلى الظلِّ المُعَرَّق
لأشجار الفُسْتُق هَرَباً من شمسٍ
تَسْفَعُ الأعشابَ التي نلهو عليها
وتُسَخِّنُ الصنابيرَ التي
تتدلّى منها رَقائقُ الثلج في الشتاء؛ ولا يعتدلُ الطقسُ
إلّا في فصلي الربيع والخريفِ
حين تتنزهُ أسرتي في الحقول
خارجَ مدينتنا التي تُدعى غالباً
أمَّ الربيعَين.

3. إحتلال

فَجْوةٌ في أحجارٍ، إناءٌ من هواءٍ، وسماءٌ
مُنَقَّطَة مثلَ جلدِ السلمون المُرَقَّطِ، وترسمُ السُحابةُ فيها
خطوطاً كجَناح طائر الحَجَل: ذلك الجَذَلُ
حَلَّقَ فينا، ذلك الأمانُ والحريةُ،
جابا معنا الأطلالَ الأثرية لمُدنٍ
— خُرساباد والحَضَر والنمرود —
بينما كان النحلُ على الشَّوكِ القرمزي مثل
الحُلي على وسادة الدبابيس، والفراشاتُ
تندفعُ بسرعةٍ فتُطرِّزُ نقوشاً شَبكيّة وترشفُ
النداوةَ من الدربِ الطينيِّ الذي نسلكُهُ
حتى نُخرجَ أنفُسَنا في آخرِ اليوم
إلى الأسِرّة في البيت، تاركينَ الماضي
المُقَوَّضَ وراءنا، والصقرَ؛ صيادَ الأعالي، فوقنا
تسوقه الرياحُ قبل المذبحةِ القادمة

أمي
Mother

ترجمة: مارغا بوركي أرتاخو، و ع. الصائغ

كانتِ الولادةُ؛ كأنهم يحفرونني
ارتفعَ بطني، على أجنحةِ البَلّين*
انطلقَ الوجعُ حولي، كملاكٍ ملطّخٍ بالدماء

ثمَّ؛ كانت ولادتُكَ

رأيتكَ بعينيَّ ذاتِهما
احتضنتُكَ، ليلَ نهارٍ؛
شرنقةً أُضيئتْ من الخلف.

في الكوت — العمارة، كنتَ قد أُستضئتَ ثانيةً
كان القمرُ قد عَكَسَكَ على أظلاع الجبلِ
عندما أوقفَ المدفعيون الأتراكُ بحرفتَكَ

سَقَطْتَ ببطءٍ، كنتَ تريقَ التقرّحَ اللونيَّ

كلّ ليلة، عندما أحلُمُ، يفوتني أن أمسكَ بكَ
عظامُكَ ريشاتٌ هشّةٌ من أفراخ ناجيةٍ
وضعتها بجانب الموقدِ، مرةً، للدِّفءِ.

هوامش المترجم:
* البلين: عظم فكّ الحوت، كان بعض النساء يستخدمنه في العهد الفكتوري، كأحزمة تشدُّ البطن لأغراض جمالية.

الآلهة تعاقبُ گلگامش بموت إنكيدو
The gods punish Gilgamesh's death

ترجمة: غسان نامق
مراجعة: ع. الصائغ

"لأولئكَ الذين يبقون، لينالهم الأسى من الآلهة" ..
ملحمة جلجامش — اللوح السابع

حين وضعتُ يدي على كتفِكَ، إلتفتَّ إليّ،
وحين التفتَّ إليَّ، رأيتُكَ غيرَ مُبتسِم،
وحين رأيتُك غيرَ مُبتسِم، علمتُ أن الآلهة ستُعاقِبُك،
وحين علمتُ أن الآلهة ستُعاقِبُك، حاولتُ استرضاءَها،
وحين حاولتُ استرضاءَها، صَمَّتْ آذانَها عَنّي،
وحين صَمَّتْ آذانَها عَنّي، علمتُ أن الأملَ مفقودٌ،
وحين علمتُ أن الأملَ مفقودٌ، طعنتُ صدري بالسكين،
وحين طعنتُ صدري بالسكين، تدفَّقَ الدمُ،
وحين تدفَّقَ الدمُ، سقطتْ دودةٌ من مِنخرِكَ،
وحين سقطتْ دودةٌ من مِنخرِكَ، إضطُرِرتُ لتَركِ جَسَدِكَ،
وحين اضطُرِرتُ لتَركِ جَسَدِكَ، هِمْتُ في البرية،
وحين هِمْتُ في البرية، حلمتُ بك،
وحين حلمتُ بك، وضعتُ يدي على كتفِكَ،
وحين وضعتُ يدي على كتفِكَ، إلتفتَّ إليّ،
وحين التفتَّ إليّ، رأيتُك غيرَ مُبتسِم.

لا سَماءَ أخرى أَرْضَتْني
No other heaven pleased me

ترجمة: غسان نامق
مراجعة: ع. الصائغ

أحياناً أُداعِبُ شَعري، مُتخَيِّلاً
يَدَ أبي موضوعةً على حدودِ الأرضِ الدافئة
أو راحَهُ مرفوعةً نحو الشمسِ

مُمسكةً حَبَّةَ بُندقٍ ناعمةً مثل وَجهٍ، لُبُّها
يَكمنُ بأمانٍ داخلَ قِشرِها حتى أفتحَها لأجدَ
الخواءَ؛ كانت المسافاتُ شاسعةً جداً

عبْرَ أرضٍ وعرةٍ وغيرِ مُستكشَفةٍ؛ أندفعُ
للأمام وأرجعُ للخلف، أسيرُ مِراراً عبْرَ
المسافةِ ذاتِها بحثاً عن نهرٍ، ضِفَّةِ نهرٍ،

خطوطِ سكةِ حديدٍ أو حتى دربِ بغلٍ، أيِّ شيءٍ
ذلك ما كان، قبلُ؛ على هذا النهج، بدلاً من مجردِ
أسماءٍ في يومياتِ الحربِ — بيت عيسى، دلي عباس،

الفلوجة —كلها بعيدةٌ ويصعبُ الوصولُ إليها
وحدهُ القمرُ؛ هو بوصلتي، أنحني عليه مُحَذِّفاً
بينما المسافةُ بيننا تتصلَّبُ وتفترُّ..

الآن؛ كما قبلُ
Now as then

ترجمة: د. تاج السر كندورة
مراجعة: ع. الصائغ

إقرأ آثارَ أقدامِنا، على الطريقِ الطويلِ، خارجَ بابل
فهي ستُخبرُكَ

كيف توقّفَ النهرُ، كيف غدتِ الأسماكُ في عُلَب
وكيف كان للهواءِ مذاقُ الرخامِ، وكيف قاتلتْ رئاتُنا كي تتنفسَ
كأنّها تحولتْ إلى حَجَرٍ..

وكيف اختفتْ عنّا أنفسُنا
في ظلالِ أشجارِ النخيلِ مسبوكة بالبرونز
على جدران قصرِ سنحاريب.

وما نزالُ في رحيلٍ؛ مثلَ أشباح غيرِ مرئيةٍ،
نُحلّقُ عبر القاراتِ، بين المطاراتِ. كلُّ مدينةٍ جديدةٍ تابوتٌ حجريٌّ
فرَّ منها الجنيُّ المجتمّعُ الذي كان يحمينا.

ودائماً هناك شذا الأرز والسرو والبقس والعرعر.
ودائماً هناك ذبابةُ مايو وهي تحوّمُ فوق الماءِ
ودائماً هناك الأمُّ والطفلُ يفارقان بلادَهما إلى الأبد.